Books by Richard Olney

SIMPLE FRENCH FOOD 1974

THE FRENCH MENU COOKBOOK 1970

Simple French Food

Earthenware poëlons *and copper* plats à sauter